A SUPER DAY AT SAMMY'S

- -

A one-act comedy for middle or high school

by
John Glass

www.studentplays.org
john@studentplays.org

<u>Copyright information. Please read!</u>

☞ About StudentPlays ☜

Student Plays consists of **John Glass, Jackie Jernigan,** and **Dominic Torres.** We are a group of playwrights and directors that have written scripts for elementary school through college. We are proud of the variety of ages that our scripts serve.

Student Plays has "creepy" plays, and we also have Latino-themed plays. These are scripts that focus on Latino youths and the Latino experience. Any school can perform a Latino-themed play: it just requires a general introduction and basic exposure to the Spanish language, something that most schools and students already have.

To learn more, visit www.studentplays.org, or to contact one of the playwrights directly, simply email us at john@studentplays.org.

A Super Day at Sammy's

☆ Characters ☆

JODI Female. Oldest sibling. Smart, confident.

MAX Male. Funny. Lives for food.

AIDEN Male. Spacey. Little common sense.

REBECCA Female. Kind. Bookworm.

MR. SHAPIRO Jodi's boss. Scattered. Bossy.

MR. DONALDSON Customer. Clueless. Zones out.

MRS. DONALDSON Customer. Quick-witted.

LOUANN Customer. Kind, passive.

LANA Customer. Sassy. Louann's sister.

The time is the present. Scenes **One** and **Three** take place in a typical living room of a house. Scene **Two** is set in a typical business office, with a basic setup of chairs or tables, a computer, etc.

JODI, MAX, AIDEN, and REBECCA are all siblings, and JODI is the oldest. The DONALDSONS, LOUANN and LANA are all adult characters, and could be performed by students (with wigs, moustaches, etc. for a comical effect) or by adult actors.

SCENE ONE

At RISE: Morning. MAX, REBECCA, AIDEN, and JODI are all in the living room of the house. MAX is at the window, watching as their parents leave for work.

MAX: Okay, hang on a minute. Wait. Wait. Wait. Okay . . . they're gone! *(Turns to the others.)*

AIDEN: So what is it, Jodi?

REBECCA: Yeah, tell us. What's the big deal?

JODI: Okay, here it is. It's not a big deal, really, but . . . I got a job.

REBECCA: What?

JODI: I got a summer job.

MAX: Where?

JODI: At a travel agency.

AIDEN: A travel agency?? Why??

JODI: How else are we gonna pay for mom and dad's anniversary gift?

MAX: I don't know. I'm cutting grass all summer!

JODI: Please . . .

AIDEN: I'm throwing newspapers.

JODI: Max, you cut *one* yard every other week. And Aiden, you throw those dumb newspapers for three hours every Friday.

AIDEN: *Four* hours, thank you very much.

JODI: Okay, *four* then. You guys can't even buy breakfast with that kind of money.

AIDEN: Yes we can!

JODI: No you can't.

MAX: Well, actually, *I* sure can't.

JODI: Come on, we talked about all this. Right?

REBECCA: Yes.

AIDEN: Sort of.

JODI: It's only for June and July, while school is out. It'll give me some spending money, and it'll help pay for Mom and Dad's gift.

AIDEN: So, what is it? A travel agency?

JODI: Yes. They help people plan their trips and vacations.

MAX: People can do that on the computer!

JODI: I know. There aren't many travel agencies left. But there are a few. This one is called "Sammy's" and he's been around forever.

AIDEN: Where is it?

JODI: It's right here, in Baytown. It's close. I can ride my bike there. It'll be every day, and I can be home before Mom and Dad get here.

MAX: What if Dad finds out? He won't like it if you're gone all day.

JODI: They're not going to find out! You guys can't say a word!! *(Pause.)* Okay??

REBECCA: Yes.

AIDEN: Okay.

MAX: Okay. *(Beat.)* Jodi, what *is* the job? What will you be doing?

JODI: I'm a secretary. I'll answer the phone, and take care of the customers that come in. I'll help plan their travel plans.

AIDEN: But what about our laundry?

REBECCA: Yeah! Who's gonna wash our clothes?

MAX: And what about our lunch? You're our big sister. Who's gonna make our lunch every day?

JODI: Stop it! This is what I'm talking about! You guys need to start taking care of yourselves. Stop being so helpless!

AIDEN: I'm not helpless!

REBECCA: Please. You can't even find the bathroom.

AIDEN: What??

JODI: I'm serious. I'm not going to be here during the daytime. You three will have to learn to do things for yourselves.

(Pause. They take this in.)

MAX: You mean . . . we have to make our own cereal?

JODI: Yes.

REBECCA: We have to start doing the vacuuming? And feeding the fish?

JODI: Yes! *Everything.* It's time you guys grew up. Max, when was the last time you unloaded the dishwasher?

MAX: Uhh . . .

JODI: Aiden, when was the last time you made lunch for everybody?

AIDEN: Uhh . . .

REBECCA: Aiden can't even boil water.

AIDEN: Yes I can!

MAX: *I* can!

REBECCA: *(To MAX.)* Nobody's talking to you.

JODI: This is my point exactly. It's high time you three gained some responsibility. Rebecca, when was the last time you stopped going through Aunt Ginger's book collection and helped cut the grass?

AIDEN: Never!

MAX: That's all she does, is read those dusty old books.

REBECCA: I like to read.

JODI: Well, goodie for you. But those books will be there forever.

MAX: Man, I hope not.

REBECCA: They're important books.

JODI: But keeping the house maintained is important too. Right? I'm serious. I'm a working girl now, and I'm not going to be here every day.

(Big pause as she takes a breath.)

AIDEN: Hmm. Well. A travel agency, huh?

JODI: Yes.

MAX: Are you going to have coffee and doughnuts in there? Like on television?

REBECCA: Max!! Be serious!

JODI: No, silly. It's not a restaurant.

MAX: Awww . . .

JODI: It's just a regular office. You know.

AIDEN: Well, it'll be kind of hard without you here to help us. But . . . I guess we'll manage.

REBECCA: Yeah.

JODI: That's what I want to hear. I'll leave the phone number here in case you guys need to reach me.

REBECCA: Okay.

MAX: Wow. Our big sister. The working girl.

AIDEN: Yep!

JODI: So . . . are you guys ready?

AIDEN: Huh?

REBECCA: Where are we going?

JODI: I told you guys. Today we're going to Charlie Cheese.

AIDEN: Yeah, baby!!

MAX: I thought you had a job!

JODI: Not until tomorrow, dummy. Today we'll eat some pizza and have some fun.

REBECCA: Great!

JODI: And then tomorrow I start work. Come on, let's go.

REBECCA: But wait! I wanted to go through some more of those books today! Especially the ones about the presidents!

JODI: Those books can wait.

MAX: Yes they can. The pizza *can't*.

JODI: Vamos. You guys ready to leave now?

REBECCA: Yes, I guess so.

AIDEN: Yippee!

MAX: Charlie Cheese, baby!

REBECCA: Charlie Cheese, it is.

JODI: *(Playfully.)* Goodness. I can't wait to leave you guys and start my job.

AIDEN: What??

JODI: Just kidding. Let's go!

(They exit. Lights fade. End of scene.)

SCENE TWO

At RISE: The office of Sammy Shapiro, morning, the next day. MR. SHAPIRO is showing JODI around.

JODI: Wow. This is all very nice.

MR. SHAPIRO: Well, thank you, thank you. We've been here for a long time. My father founded the business years ago and we are proud to serve the community. *(With attitude and irritation.)* Even *if* the Internet has wiped most of the industry out . . .

JODI: Oh.

MR. SHAPIRO: So, here is your desk.

JODI: Okay.

MR. SHAPIRO: And as I told you, coffee is very important. Please give all of our customers a nice warm cup of coffee. And here is the phone. We do a lot of business over the phone so telephone skills are crucial.

JODI: Okay.

MR. SHAPIRO: It's very important that you always answer the phone just like this. *(Picks up receiver.)*

"It's a super day at Sammy's Travel Agency! How can I help you??" *(Looks back at her, then hangs up.)* Got it?

JODI: Yes.

MR. SHAPIRO: Just like that. Now, you try.

JODI: Uh, okay. *(She picks up the receiver.)* It's a super day at Sammy's Travel Agency!

MR. SHAPIRO: Perfect! Exactly like that! Very good. *(He checks his cell.)* Uh, I kind of need to take this call. You go ahead, Jodi, and get settled, and get acquainted with everything. I'll be in my office, and throughout the day I'll be bringing in some documents for you to file.

JODI: Okay. Sounds good.

MR. SHAPIRO: And remember: don't let me down!

JODI: Yes sir!

> *(She sits and he begins to exit, while talking on his phone.)*

MR. SHAPIRO*:* Hi, honey-bear. *(Pause.)* What? *(Pause.)* Why, yes, I did, honey-bear, I did! *(Pause.)* But sweet-cakes, I thought I did! Oh, I'm sorry.

(Exits. Long pause as JODI sits and gets comfortable. The phone rings, and she answers.)

JODI: It's a super day at Sammy's Travel Agency! *(Pause.)* Max? What is it??

(Pause. The DONALDSONS enter.)

JODI: No, no. Max, you have to open the end of the bag and then put it in the microwave.
  (Pause.)
Right. Right. For 45 seconds.
  (Pause.)
Right. Okay, got it? Bye.
  (Hangs up. Looks at the DONALDSONS.)
Good morning! Welcome to Sammy's.

MRS. DONALDSON: Thank you.

MR. DONALDSON: Hello.

JODI: Can I help you guys?

MRS. DONALDSON: Well, we'd like to plan a trip.

JODI: Okay, great!

MR. DONALDSON: To Argentina.

JODI: Sounds good! Just have a seat right there, and we'll get you guys started.

MRS. DONALDSON: Thank you.

MR. DONALDSON: Thanks.

JODI: You're very welcome. *(Beat.)* Okay . . . so you want to go to Argentina, huh?

MR. DONALDSON: That's right.

JODI: Going to speak a little Spanish, are you?

MRS. DONALDSON: Uh, yes. I suppose. We want to go during March. From the 15th to the 25th, if possible.

JODI: *(Typing on computer.)* Okay, here we go. March. The 15th to the 25th. Hmmm.
 (The phone rings.)
Excuse me, guys. Sorry.
 (She picks up.)
It's a super day at Sammy's Travel Agency!
 (Pause.)
Rebecca, what do you want?
 (Pause.)
Oh, those ridiculous books!
 (To the Donaldsons.)
It's my sister. We just inherited all these books, and my sister's been going through them. Crazy.
 (Back on the phone.)
No, no, no. I told you: you can put the ones you've already gone through in that red box. In the washroom.

(Pause.)
Right. Stick them in there. In the washroom. Okay?
Okay, bye.
(Hangs up.)
That girl is hardheaded. Okay, now, where were we?

MRS. DONALDSON: We want to book a trip to Argentina. *(With slight exasperation.)* Remember?

JODI: Yes, I do remember! Argentina. Um, is that by chance near Alabama??

MR. DONALDSON: No!

> *(Enter Mr. Shapiro, carrying a large stack of papers.)*

JODI: Oh, just kidding! Sorry. Okay, back to work. Let me get those dates typed in and see what we can find.

MR. SHAPIRO: Hi there!

MR. DONALDSON: Hello.

MR. SHAPIRO: I'm Sammy Shapiro, how are you? *(Extends hand, and vigorously shakes theirs.)*

MRS. DONALDSON*:* We're fine, thank you.

MR. SHAPIRO*:* Great, great. I trust that Jodi is taking good care of you two . . ?

MRS. DONALDSON: Yes, um, so far.

MR. SHAPIRO: Jodi, you didn't offer them any coffee??

JODI: Oh, I was going to, sorry.

MR. SHAPIRO: Come, come, they must have coffee *(Begins to pour two cups.)*

MRS. DONALDSON*:* Really, we're fine. We just want to plan our trip.

MR. SHAPIRO: Nonsense, coffee is essential. Coffee is good! One cup for each of you!! Now, where are you folks vacationing to?

MR. DONALDSON: Argentina.

MR. SHAPIRO: Argentina! Ah! The land of the quesadilla.

MRS. DONALDSON: No, actually, that's *Mexico*.

MR. SHAPIRO: Ah, whatever. *(Sees that he has a call on his phone.)* Oh, I must take this. Um, Jodi?

JODI: Yes?

MR. SHAPIRO: *(Pointing.)* Your papers are right there to file. And take care of our customers, okay?

JODI: Yes sir!

MR. SHAPIRO: Make sure they are comfortable! I must take this phone call. *(Answers his phone, begins to exit.)* Darling, I told you about these little phone calls while I'm at work. *(Pause.)* I know, I know . . . but honey-bun, I took care of that . . .

    (Exits.)

MRS. DONALDSON: *(Impatiently.)* We'd like your best rate possible. We need two tickets for a round-trip flight.

JODI: Round-trip, got it. Here we go. Okay. March 10th through the 20th.

MRS. DONALDSON: No, that's the 15th through the 25th.

JODI: Oh, right! My fault! Okay, pulling the numbers up right now.
    (The phone rings.)
Gosh, I'm so sorry. One moment, please.
    (Picks up.)
It's a super day at Sammy's Travel Agency! How can I help you?
    (Pause.)
Aiden, what is it now??
    (Pause.)
What? The TV? No, no, you have to push the power button first, then the cable button.

(Looks back at the DONALDSONS.)
Silly boy can't work the remote control.
(Back on phone.)
Okay, you got it? No, the *power* button first, the *cable* button second. Right. Okay, enough with the phone calls!! Bye!
(Hangs up.)
Okay!

MRS. DONALDSON: Uh, miss, could we please get on with planning our trip??

JODI: Yes, yes, of course! I apologize. Okay, back to the computer. Here we go. We are going to Alabama.

MR. DONALDSON: Argentina!!

(Enter LOUANN and LANA.)

JODI: Right, right! Sorry! *Argentina.* Okay. My fault! *(Beat. She notices LOUANN and LANA, and stands to welcome them.)* Oh, hello!

LOUANN: Hi.

JODI: Come right in, come right in.

LANA*:* Thank you.

JODI: You guys can just have a seat right here.

LANA: Great. Um, we'd like somebody to help us plan a trip to Alabama.

JODI: Oh! We were just talking about Alabama!

LOUANN: Were you?

JODI: Yes!

LOUANN: Interesting.

> *(Enter Mr. Shapiro, with another stack of papers that he places on the desk.)*

LANA: That *is* interesting.

JODI: Yep, Alabama. Well, you two can just sit and relax—

MR. SHAPIRO: Um, Jodi? Aren't you taking care of *those* customers first??

JODI: Yes, Mr. Shapiro, I was just getting these guys seated.

MR. SHAPIRO: And where is their coffee??

JODI: Oh, right, the coffee.

MR. SHAPIRO: All of our customers need coffee!

LANA: We're fine, sir. We don't drink coffee.

MR. SHAPIRO: Well, okay. Chop-chop, Jodi! Be sure that everybody here is satisfied.

JODI: Yes sir!

MR. SHAPIRO: You folks don't worry. She will take good care of all of you. *(Beat. Sees that he has a call. Begins to exit.)* Oh, I must get this call. Okay, Jodi, make me proud! *(On his phone.)* Hi, blossom-cakes. *(Pause.)* Yes, yes! When? I love that restaurant's meat loaf!

> *(He exits.)*

JODI*:* Okay, back to Argentina. Not Alabama!

LANA: Uh, well, *we* actually wanted to go to Alabama.

JODI: Oh, I know. I just, you know, was making a joke.

LOUANN: We'd like to go sometime during February. During Mardi Gras.

JODI: Oh. *(Confused.)* During February?

LANA: Yes.

JODI: Okay. Let me write that down really quick.

MRS. DONALDSON: Excuse me. Weren't *we* here first?

JODI: Yes! I was just writing down their destination. That's all.

LANA: All we were doing was reminding her of where we wanted to go.

MRS. DONALDSON: Well, it sure sounded like you were trying to skip us.

LANA: Skip you??!

MRS. DONALDSON: Yes.

JODI: Well, hang on guys, I'm going to take care of *all* of you.

LANA: We weren't trying to skip anybody!

LOUANN: I knew we should have purchased this trip on the Internet.

MR. DONALDSON: *(Pointing to MRS. DONALDSON.)* That's what I told *her*!

MRS. DONALDSON: Oh, I don't like that thing. It's confusing.

LANA: *(Pointing to LOUANN.)* That's what I told *her*!

MRS. DONALDSON: Um, can we get back to our trip please??

(Enter MR. SHAPIRO, carrying more papers.)

JODI: Yes.

LANA: Boy, you sure are in a hurry to get down to Argentina. What's wrong? Are you running from something?

MRS. DONALDSON: I beg your pardon??

LANA: You heard me. Bonnie and Clyde, running off to South America.

LOUANN: Whaat??

MR. DONALDSON: *(Dreamily.)* Bonnie and Clyde. *That* was a great movie!

JODI: Oh, can you guys please not argue??

MRS. DONALDSON: Who's arguing? I was just trying to tell them that we were here first!!

MR. SHAPIRO: Excuse me!! Just what's going on here?? Jodi . . ?

JODI: I'm so sorry, Mr. Shapiro. I'm only trying to help everybody and—

MRS. DONALDSON: Sir, my husband and I were here before *they* were, and we're still sitting here, waiting to plan our trip!

JODI: And I'll do it for you! I have the prices for Alabama, right here on my computer!

MR. DONALDSON: That's *Argentina*, not Alabama!

JODI: Oh, right!

MRS. DONALDSON: How many times do you need to be told? *(Sarcastically.)* Hmmpph. *Alabama.*

LANA: What's wrong with Alabama? *(To LOUANN.)* See, I was right. They *are* like Bonnie and Clyde.

MR. DONALDSON: What a movie!

MRS. DONALDSON: Ohhh!

MR. SHAPIRO: Okay, now, everybody settle down! Please! Just settle down!
    (Pause as everybody quietens.)
Now, listen, Jodi, you have *got* to tighten up! These customers are counting on you!

JODI: I know. I'm sorry.

MR. SHAPIRO: Folks, I assure you, you will get the service that you need.

LANA: I hope so!

MR. SHAPIRO: I promise. Right, Jodi?

JODI: Yes, Mr. Shapiro.

MR. SHAPIRO: Okay. *(Checking his phone.)* I would stay and help you all but I must take this important call. So sorry! *(On his phone.)* Hold on, honey bun. *(To JODI.)* Okay, I must go. Back to it, Joanna! Do a good job!

JODI: Yes sir.

    (He exits.)

JODI: Okay, I'm pulling up the numbers now. Let's see . . . Argentina. Okay, it's loading . . . here we are. *(Beat. She stares at the computer screen.)* Oh. Wow, I'm afraid that there aren't any morning flights possible.

MRS. DONALDSON: *(Disappointed.)* Oh.

JODI: There's a flight available at noon.

MR. DONALDSON: But we wanted to go in the morning.

MRS. DONALDSON: Right.

JODI: I'm sorry.

LANA: Goodness, we'll be here all day.

MRS. DONALDSON: *(To LANA.)* Um, excuse me . . ?

JODI: I'm really sorry but that's all I have right now.

LANA: You heard the girl. That's all she has. We don't have all this time, you know.

MRS. DONALDSON: Good Lord, you two sure are in a hurry to get down to *Alabama*. To *Mardi Gras*!

LANA: What??

MRS. DONALDSON: You heard me! And whoever heard of Mardi Gras in Alabama?

LANA: Uh, Mardi Gras *began* in Alabama, genius.

MRS. DONALDSON: Who are you calling a genius?

MR. DONALDSON: *(Sarcastically.)* You're telling me.

JODI: Guys, stop! Look, I just found a flight to Argentina at eleven-thirty in the morning. Will that work?

LANA: My uncle Jessie was born in Alabama. In Mobile. And he ought to know.

LOUANN: Uncle Jessie. He was one weird character.

LANA: What??

LOUANN: It's true, Lana. That man thought he was the best house painter in the South. Good grief. Old codger.

JODI: Will that work for you all? Eleven-thirty?

LANA: Old codger? Louann, that's *your* uncle too!

JODI: Can we please focus here?

MRS. DONALDSON: *They're* the ones that started it.

LANA: I beg your pardon?

MRS. DONALDSON: It's true.

MR. DONALDSON: How do you beg someone's pardon?

LANA: Ohhh!!

(The phone rings.)

JODI: Uh, sorry. One moment.

MRS. DONALDSON: More like one-*hundred* moments.

JODI: It's a super day at Sammy's Travel Agency!
    (Pause.)
Max? No, let me call you back. I can't talk right now!
    (Pause.)
What? No, no, no. I told you guys, Mom put the coconut cream pie in that middle drawer in the fridge, at the very back. Not on the top shelf like she normally does.

MRS. DONALDSON: I can't believe this.

MR. DONALDSON: You're telling me.

JODI: No! In the *middle drawer*! And what are you three doing, eating pie? It's too early in the day for that!

MRS. DONALDSON: *(Standing.)* Honey, let's go. I've had enough.

JODI: Wait a minute, ma'am!

MR. DONALDSON: Yeah, wait a minute. I still want to hear about the coconut cream pie.

MRS. DONALDSON: *(Yanking his arm.)* Come on, Larry! We are done with this place!

JODI: But . . ! *(Back on the phone.)* No, not you, Max. I didn't call you a butt! *(Looks back at her.)* Mrs. . . . ?

MRS. DONALDSON: Good day!!

MR. DONALDSON: But Olivia . . !

MRS. DONALDSON: *(Yanking him harder.)* Come on, Larry!!

> *(They exit abruptly.)*

JODI: Max. I have to hang up. Bye! *(Slams phone down. She calls out.)* Hello? Guys . . ? *(Pause as she turns to the others.)* Ladies, I'm so sorry for all that.

LANA: Goodness.

JODI: I'm gonna take care of you guys right now.

LOUANN: We sure hope so!

JODI: Okay, I'm typing in the information. Let's see . . . round-trip tickets to Albania.

LANA: Alabama!

JODI: Oh, sorry!

LANA: Not Argentina! Not Albania! *Alabama*!

JODI: Okay! Got it. I know!

LANA: Well, apparently you *don't* know!

LOUANN: Give her a break. At least those other two scoundrels left.

LANA: Oh, be quiet, Louann! What do *you* know??

LOUANN: I know that you're wrong about Uncle Jessie. That old bird drove me crazy!

(The phone rings.)

JODI: Oh! Hang on one moment, please.

LANA: Not again!

JODI: It's a super day at Sammy's Travel Agency!

LANA: This isn't working.

JODI: Aiden! What *is* it? *(Pause.)* No, no! To make the scooter go, you have to pull the black lever up and push the red lever down.

LANA: Uh, miss . . ?

JODI: What? No, that's just some old lady here in the office.

LANA: Excuse me??

JODI: *(To LANA.)* I'm sorry, ma'am, you know what I mean.

LOUANN: She called you an old lady. Ha!

JODI: No, Aiden. The *black* lever has to go up. The *red* lever down.

LANA: That does it! Let's go Louann. *(Stands.)*

LOUANN: Wait! This is just beginning to get good.

LANA: Come on! *(Yanks her arm, begins to exit.)*

JODI: Ladies, please don't leave! *(Back on the phone.)* Aiden, I have to go!

LANA: I am calling the Better Business Bureau on this place!

JODI: Good bye! *(Slams phone down.)* Ladies . .??

LOUANN: The Better Business Bureau?? Ha, are they still in business?

JODI: Ladies???

(They exit. A pause as she stands in complete disbelief. The phone rings, and she turns to answer it, in absolute fury.)

JODI: Hello?? What is it?? I told you three morons: stop calling up here!! You've been calling me all morning!

> *(Pause. She realizes it's a customer. Enter MR. SHAPIRO. Her back is to him as she speaks.)*

JODI: Oh. Oh. I am so sorry. Oh my gosh . . yes, this is Sammy's Travel Agency. *(Pause.)* What? No, I didn't mean that! I'm sorry! You see, my siblings have been calling my job all morning and . . . um. Okay. Okay. Yes. Good bye.

> *(She hangs up, and turns to see him.)*

MR. SHAPIRO: Jodi?

JODI: Yes?

MR. SHAPIRO: Was that a customer on the phone?

JODI: Um. Yes.

MR. SHAPIRO: And . . . where are the customers that were just here??

JODI: Um . . . they left.

MR. SHAPIRO: They left?

JODI: Yes.

MR. SHAPIRO: All of them?

JODI: Yes. I'm sorry, Mr. Shapiro. Oh, I'm so sorry.

MR. SHAPIRO: Well. I'm afraid this isn't going to work out, Jodi.

JODI: I . . . know.

> *(Pause. She is sad and dejected.)*

MR. SHAPIRO: I really thought you would be a good addition to my office. But . . .

JODI: I know. I really messed up.

MR. SHAPIRO: *(Extending his hand, which she takes.)* Well . . . good-bye.

JODI: Bye, Mr. Shapiro. I really am sorry.

MR. SHAPIRO: I appreciate your efforts.

JODI: Thank you.

MR. SHAPIRO: And I wish you all the best.

JODI: Thanks.

> *(She turns to leave, deflated. The phone suddenly rings. He picks up the receiver.)*

MR. SHAPIRO: Um, hello! It's a super day at Sammy's Travel Agency!

JODI: *(As she walks out.)* If you say so!!

　　　　(She exits as MR. SHAPIRO continues talking on the phone. Lights fade to black. End of scene.)

SCENE THREE

At RISE: The living room of the house, a few hours later. REBECCA, MAX, and AIDEN are all busy doing various things, and JODI has just walked through the front door, carrying her backpack or purse. A pie is on the kitchen/dining room table.

REBECCA: Jodi! You're home early.

MAX: Hey! How did it go?

JODI: How did it go? How did it go? How do you guys think it went? I got fired.

AIDEN: What?

JODI: I got fired! It didn't work out.

REBECCA: Huh?

AIDEN: What do you mean?

JODI: It was horrible. Oh, it was *beyond* horrible! I had four customers all at once, and they were all talking at the same time, and arguing!

REBECCA: Wow.

JODI: But do you know what the main thing was? You guys kept calling me! And it got me in trouble!

AIDEN: What??

MAX: We didn't call you *that* much!

JODI: Please. Aiden, *you* called for that silly scooter. And I've told you a million times how to work that thing.

AIDEN: Well . . .

JODI: And Rebecca, you called to ask me where to put those books!

REBECCA: Only one time!

JODI: Oh man, the phone kept ringing over and over. Max, what's your problem? You couldn't even find the pie by yourself??

MAX: I didn't know where it was! And I was hungry!

JODI: Oh, the whole thing was terrible. The customers, the telephone, my grouchy boss . . . it was one big train wreck.

REBECCA: We're sorry, Jodi.

AIDEN: Yeah.

JODI: These two people came in, wanting to plan a trip to Alabama, and—

AIDEN: Alabama?

MAX: Where's that?

JODI: It doesn't matter. Another couple wanted to go to Argentina.

REBECCA: Argentina?

AIDEN: Where's that?

JODI: It DOESN'T MATTER!! *(Pause.)* What matters is that I got fired! And you guys were the reason that I got canned!

MAX: We really are sorry. But we needed your help!

JODI: I told you birdbrains you had to start taking care of yourselves! Goodness. The *scooter*!

AIDEN: That thing is hard to figure out!

JODI: Those *dusty old books*! The *pie*! Is there anything here you can guys *can* do?

> *(Pause. They all look at her, somewhat stunned.)*

REBECCA*:* Sorry, Jodi.

AIDEN*:* Yeah, we're sorry.

REBECCA: I feel bad.

AIDEN: *(Suddenly.)* Oh, wait! Rebecca, tell her what happened!

MAX: Yes, tell her!

JODI: Tell me what?

REBECCA: Well . . . there actually *are* some things that we can do.

JODI: What happened? What are you guys talking about?

REBECCA: You know those books that aunt Ginger left us?

JODI: Those raggedy old books, yes. The ones you *called* me about. What about them?

REBECCA: Well, in those raggedy old books . . . I found 200 dollars!

JODI: What?

REBECCA: Yep. It was stuck in the back of a book about Richard Nixon.

MAX: You mean *Harry Truman*.

REBECCA: No, numbskull, I mean *Nixon.* I'm the one who found it, I ought to know.

JODI: You found . . . 200 dollars?

REBECCA: Yes!

AIDEN: A gift from the ghost of aunt Ginger!

REBECCA: Stop it, Aiden.

JODI: Well, maybe it *is* a gift from aunt Ginger. Or at least, a gift from the presidents. 200 bucks will certainly cover the cost of mom and dad's anniversary gift.

MAX: Yep.

JODI: That's more than enough. *(Pause.)* Wow. 200 dollars.

AIDEN: Isn't that great? And maybe we can buy something for ourselves with the money left over.

MAX: Yes! A year's supply of coconut cream pie!

AIDEN: Video games!

REBECCA: Guys, quit. We aren't buying anything extra with that money. Just the gift for mom and dad.

JODI: This is all so bizarre. I get fired. And you guys find money.

REBECCA: Well, actually, *I* found the money.

MAX: *(Mocking her.)* "Well, actually, I found the money."

AIDEN: So . . . are you still mad at us, sis?

JODI: Hmmm.

MAX: Yeah, this makes it okay, right?

JODI: It doesn't make it okay, no. You guys still cost me my job. You three still need to take care of yourselves. *(Beat.)* But . . .

REBECCA: But what?

JODI: I guess it's not that bad.

AIDEN: Hooray! She's not mad at us anymore!

JODI: Not so fast! Hang on a minute!

MAX: No, you just said that you weren't mad anymore!

JODI: I didn't exactly say *that*!

MAX: Yes you did.

AIDEN: Yep! And look on the bright side, Jodi. Sure, you lost your job, and that's too bad. But we are 200 dollars richer!

REBECCA: Right! We can now buy the anniversary gift. And you don't have to work anymore!

AIDEN: No more being all serious and all professional.

MAX: Right! No more of those annoying customers!

AIDEN: That want to go *Alaska*!

JODI: Alabama!

AIDEN: Wherever.

JODI: Actually, it was Alabama *and* Argentina.

REBECCA: No more "it's a super day at Sammy's!" Every time we called you, you answered the phone that way.

JODI: You guys listen carefully: I NEVER want to hear that again!

MAX: Hear what? "It's a super day at Sammy's"?

JODI: Yes. NEVER again! GOT IT??

MAX, **REBECCA** & **AIDEN**: Yes.

JODI: Okay. That settles that.

REBECCA: Ha, I don't blame you, Jodi. You must have gotten sick of saying that.

JODI: Oh, you have no clue. *(Notices the pie on the table.)* Well, that's that. I see you guys left the pie out. Is there enough left?

MAX: Yep! I was about eat another slice.

JODI: Okay. Well, let's all sit down and have a piece. Then we can talk about mom and dad's anniversary gift.

AIDEN: Ah man, this is great. Jodi, I never thought I'd say this. But . . . it's good to have you home again.

REBECCA: Yeah!

MAX: And not mad at us anymore!

AIDEN: Exactly.

JODI: Don't push it. I just got here.

REBECCA: We're going to try harder to take care of ourselves, Jodi.

JODI: Promise?

REBECCA: We promise.

MAX: No more asking you to always make our lunch.

AIDEN: No more asking you to help us with our video games or toys.

JODI: Well, that's more like it.

AIDEN: No more working!!

MAX: No more "it's a super day at Sammy's"!!

JODI: *(Lunging at him.)* Okay, let me at him!

MAX: What??

JODI: Come here, Max!

MAX: Ohh! I forgot!! Sorry!

JODI: *(Picks up the pie, threatens him with it.)* Want some pie, Max??

AIDEN: Jodi, all he said was "a super day at Sammy's"!!

MAX: Yeah!

JODI: Oh, *you* want some too, huh?

AIDEN: No!!

REBECCA: Calm down, Jodi!

JODI: I'm gonna get both of them!! *(Chasing them around the table.)* I told you guys!!

AIDEN: Take it easy, Jodi!!

REBECCA: Yeah!

JODI: Come here!!

MAX: *(Taunting her.)* A super day at Sammy's! A super day at Sammy's!!

AIDEN: *(Joining in.)* A super day at Sammy's!

> *(They continue to chant this and taunt her as she chases them with the pie. REBECCA looks on in horror. Lights fade. End of play.)*

☞ **More from Student Plays** ☜

Othello's Just Another Fellow

Dramedy. **Grades 5-7.** 25-35 minutes. 8 actors: 4 males, 3 females, one teacher (or student portraying a teacher) 3 to 5 extras, if needed. ****A Latino-themed play****

A group of students are involved in a school production of *Othello*, but one of them is disturbed about the lack of diversity in the play. He takes certain steps to disrupt the play but in the end is encouraged by the others to try and make a difference in another, more constructive way. A lesson is learned, and the production is saved from disaster!

Pagasqueeny's Pantry

Comedy. **Middle/High School.** 15-20 minutes. 6 actors: 3 females, 2 males. One student (or a teacher) plays the comical role of the elderly Mr. Pagasqueeny.

Three friends sneak into Mr. Pagasqueeny's home to get something that one of them left behind. But in walks Pagasqueeny and they must hide in the pantry! In this comical play, a lesson is learned about honesty and trust, but it takes a heated discussion in the pantry and a subsequent attempt to escape to find this out!

Una Carta de Abuelo

Dramedy. **Middle/High School.** 35-45 minutes. 10 actors: 1 teacher, 5 females, 4 males. (With the option of 4-5 extra actors in two scenes.) ****A Latino-themed play****

Two cousins discover an old letter in their late grandfather's comic collection that they think leads to treasure! The cousins often butt heads, with one believing that he is more "Mexican," the other believing that some people make too much of a fuss about "being Mexican." Thus, they form their *own* groups in search of what Grandpa hid long ago. But what they find is actually worth more than merely silver or gold.

Barbecue at the Prom!

Dramedy. **Grades 5-8.** 25-35 minutes. 6 actors: 3 females, 3 males

It's a classic tale of guys versus girls! It's a prom committee, and everybody is supposed to work together but differences and opinions get in the way, causing the guys and girls to form their groups. For the end-of-the-year prom, one side wants pasta and lace, the other wants sports and barbecue! The two groups square off but eventually work together, demonstrating the importance of cooperation and compromise.

Going to Guatemala

Dramedy. **High School.** 50-60 minutes. 11 actors. 6 males, 5 females.   ****A Latino-themed play****

A Latino student is chosen at the last minute to join a humanitarian group from his school that is headed to Guatemala. But since his Spanish is weak, he faces ridicule and criticism from certain peers. Jealousy and anger trickle throughout the campus as the trip approaches, and the social buzz of the high school becomes even more hectic when the student's trip money is stolen on campus, jeopardizing his trip.

Stravinsky's Kitchen

Comedy. **High School/College.** 12-15 minutes. 3 actors: 3 males (or females).

Two friends secretly enter the home of an employer to obtain a forgotten object but the homeowner abruptly arrives home while they are there. As they hide in the kitchen's pantry and plot their getaway, the two talk and eventually argue, exposing the true colors of one of them. Upon their hasty exit a mistake is made, and one of them capitalizes on this mistake, resulting in his/her fortune.

Forty Whacks

Drama. Spooky. **High School/College.** 25-35 minutes. 3 actors: 2 females, 1 male.

A pair of siblings have inherited the Lizzie Borden Bed and Breakfast in New England. Although the business was run for decades in a quiet, respectable fashion, one of the siblings is over-ambitious, wanting to unearth an alleged piece of buried evidence within the house. This brings about a chilly uneasiness between brother and sister, and perhaps within the house itself.

John Calhoun and a Thief

Drama. **College.** 35-40 minutes. 3 actors: 2 females, 1 male.

Kicked out of a university PhD program, a bitter and dejected female lifts from the library archives original copies of John Calhoun's personal documents. Counseled and consoled by her roommates, her conscience slowly gets to her; but as she seeks entry to other universities her luck turns to worse, and the subsequent decisions she makes regarding the historic papers cause this one-act play to become darker, if not funnier.

Honoring the Hijacker

Drama. **College.** 12-15 minutes. 4 actors: 2 females, 2 males.

It's 1981, the ten-year anniversary of the famed hijacker D.B. Cooper. The play's four characters are attending a "D.B. Festival" and have stayed up very late, outlasting everybody else. The late night chit-chat goes from pranks and jokes to outright volatility, and suddenly this get-together becomes something that three of the four characters didn't bargain for.

It's a Super Day at Sammy's!

Comedy. **Middle or High School.** 35-40 minutes. 9 actors: 5 females, 4 males (4 possible adults).

Jodi has found a summer job at a travel agency. But her three younger siblings can't seem to live without her! They call her at the office incessantly, which interferes with the work. The standard telephone greeting "It's a super day at Sammy's!" becomes a repeated theme of this comedy, as Jodi struggles to reach a balance between her job and her nagging siblings

Three Tenners

Comedy/Drama. **Elementary through High School.** Three Ten-Minute Plays.

Three Creepy Plays

Drama. **Middle School through College.** Three short 'creepy' plays.

Hockey Masks in Hueytown

Drama. Spooky. **High School/College.** 20-25
minutes. 4 actors: 2 males, 2 females.

Driving home for Thanksgiving break, four college
students stop off in a small rural town to retrieve one
of the student's old family pictures. They reluctantly
enter the empty home of his deceased uncle, a former
producer for the Friday the 13th movies. Strange
objects are found during their search . . but when a
hockey mask surfaces, everything really goes
sideways.

The Witch Makes Five

Drama. Spooky. **High School.** 10 minutes. 4 actors: 2
males, 2 females.

After a bizarre group camping trip, a student is
checked into a youth mental facility . When she is
visited by the other members of the trip, memories of
the weekend trickle out . . . and horrific things begin to
happen.

Mrs. Calapooza and the Culebra

Dramedy. **Grades 5-8.** 10 minutes. 5 actors: 3 females, 2 males.

Fed up with their grouchy teacher's classroom ways, four students complain and bicker back and forth during a Spanish quiz. The situation grows worse when the friends discover that one of them has pulled the ultimate prank on the teacher.

Raiders of the Lost Rakasa

Dramedy. **Grades 5-8.** 10 minutes. 7 actors: 4 females, 3 males.

Seven young explorers arrive at a cave in a far-off land in search of the great "Rakasa." They find what they want . . . along with a few of the cave's unexpected surprises.